The Ultimate
Gorilla
Book for Kids

100+ Gorilla Facts,
Photos, Quiz & More

BELLANOVA

MELBOURNE · SOFIA · BERLIN

Copyright © 2023 by Jenny Kellett

The Ultimate Gorilla Book
www.bellanovabooks.com

ISBN: 978-619-7695-92-2
Imprint: Bellanova Books

Contents

Gorillas: The Basics **6**

Western Gorilla **18**

    Western lowland gorilla *20*

    Cross River gorilla *24*

Eastern Gorilla **28**

    Eastern lowland gorilla *31*

    Mountain gorilla *35*

From birth to adulthood **38**

Their daily lives **46**

Famous gorillas **56**

The Future **64**

Other Fun Facts **70**

Gorilla Quiz **76**

    Quiz Answers **81**

Word Search Puzzle 82

Sources *85*

Introduction

Gorillas are one of the world's most beloved creatures. Not only are they cute, but their similarities to humans are so intriguing.

In this book we will learn more about the Earth's largest primate — fun facts about their lifestyle, diet and habitats, as well as the dangers that they face.

At the end, you can test your knowledge in the **Gorilla Quiz**. Are you ready? *Let's go....!*

Gorillas: The Basics

What are gorillas and where do they live?

Gorillas are great apes. Great apes are a family of primates that include eight different living species: **Pongo** (the Bornean, Sumatran and Tapanuli orangutan), **Gorilla** (eastern and western gorilla), **Pan** (the common chimpanzee and the bonobo) and **Homo** (us - humans!).

• • •

Gorillas are the largest living non-human primates.

A mountain gorilla enjoying a snack in Uganda.

There are two species of gorilla: **western** and **eastern**; and within these, two subspecies. We will look at each of them shortly.

• • •

Gorillas live in the tropical forests of central sub-Saharan Africa.

• • •

Gorillas share between 95-99 per cent of the same DNA as humans! However, chimpanzees and bonobos are even more closely related to us.

Gorillas are huge! They can reach heights of up to 5.9 ft (1.8 m) and weigh between 220-600 lbs (100-270 kg).

• • •

Gorillas live in groups called **troops**.

• • •

Every troop has a leader, which is called a **silverback**.

• • •

In the wild, gorillas live for between 35-40 years. In captivity, they live between 40-50 years.

The silverback has lots of responsibilities. He protects his troop from predators, mediates any conflicts and decides what they will do and where they will go each day.

The oldest ever gorilla was a Western lowland gorilla called Fatou living at Berlin Zoo. She was 62 years old.

• • •

The word 'gorilla' comes from the ancient explorer Hanno the Navigator, who discovered what they thought were hairy women in today's Sierra Leone. The Ancient Greek word for hairy women is Γόριλλαι, or *gorillaï*.

• • •

Chimpanzees, humans and gorillas all had a common ancestor 7 million years ago before each started to evolve into what we know today.

There was only one type of gorilla until after the last Ice Age.

• • •

Gorilla's hands and feet are much like ours. Their fingers and thumbs move in the same way and they can use them to grab things.

• • •

Adult male gorillas have grey backs, which is where they get the name 'silverback' from. The older they are, the lighter and more pronounced the grey becomes.

Young male gorillas are called *black backs* as they haven't yet got their grey fur.

• • •

There is no special name for female gorillas.

• • •

Gorillas are incredibly smart. Many captive gorillas have learnt to use sign language to communicate with humans.

• • •

Now, let's take a closer look at the different species and subspecies of gorilla.

WESTERN GORILLA

Scientific name: *Gorilla gorilla*

The western gorilla is the most common species. They were first formally recognized and described by American naturalist Thomas Savage in 1847.

There are two subspecies of western gorilla: **western lowland gorilla** and **Cross River gorilla**. Both species of western gorilla are critically endangered.

Although they both live in western Africa, there are plenty of differences, which we will look at now.

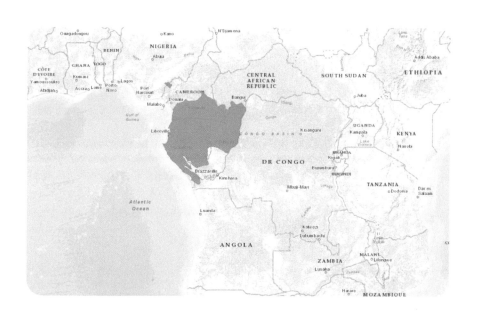

Range of the Western Gorilla (both species).

Source: IUCN Red List of Threatened Species

A female and juvenile Western lowland gorilla. Photo by Greg Hume

Western Lowland Gorilla

Scientific name: *Gorilla gorilla gorilla*

Western lowland gorillas are the smallest species of gorilla.

They live in the rainforests and swampland areas of central Africa.

Because they live in very remote places, no one knows exactly how many of them live in the wild.

In the last 20-25 years, the population of western lowland gorillas has decreased by 60%.

Gorillas aren't immune to disease, and during the 2002-2003 Ebola crisis, many western lowland gorillas died from Ebola. In one conservation park, the population decreased from 377 to 38 gorillas. It was because of this outbreak that the species went from being endangered to critically endangered.

If you have ever seen a gorilla in a zoo, it was most likely the western lowland gorilla, as no other species can be kept in a zoo. There are only very few exceptions.

They have smaller ears and wider skulls than other species. They also have greyish hair with auburn bellies.

Cross River Gorilla

Scientific name: *Gorilla gorilla diehli*

Cross River gorillas live in the forests and mountains along the border between Cameroon and Nigeria. They get their name from the Cross River that they live near. They are the most western and northern gorillas and they live around 300km (190 mi) from the nearest population of western lowland gorillas.

The Cross River gorilla was only formally recognized as a different subspecies in 2000. They are the rarest great ape in the world.

A Cross River gorilla in Primate Sanctuary Reserve, Cameroon.

Photo by Fkamtoh

Nyango, the only known Cross River gorilla in captivity. She died on October 10, 2016.

Photo by Julie Langford

Sadly, there are only an estimated 250 mature Cross River gorillas living today.

Compared with western lowland gorillas, they have smaller mouths and shorter skulls — but are otherwise very similar in size and weight.

Cross River gorillas usually live in troops of between 4-7 others — with a mix of male and females.

Not a lot is known about Cross River gorillas. However, in 2020, conservationists caught several adults and young Cross River gorillas on camera, which gave them hope for their future.

EASTERN GORILLAS

Scientific name: *Gorilla beringei*

There are two subspecies of eastern gorillas: the eastern lowland gorilla and the mountain gorilla. They are critically endangered, with their numbers declining each year.

There is only one zoo outside of their native range that has a captive eastern gorilla — Antwerp Zoo in Belgium, so the best place to see them is in the wild.

They have large heads with flat noses and huge nostrils.

Range of the Eastern Gorilla

Source: IUCN Red List of Threatened Species

A silverback eastern lowland gorilla in
Kahuzi-Biega National Park. *Photo by Joe Mckenna*

Eastern Lowland Gorilla

Scientific name: *Gorilla beringei graueri*

The eastern lowland gorilla is also known as **Grauer's gorilla**. They can only be found in the wild in the tropical rainforests of the Democratic Republic of Congo. An estimated 3,800 eastern lowland gorillas are living in the wild, much less than the western lowland gorilla. Since the mid-1990s, their numbers have declined by 50 per cent.

Of all the gorilla subspecies, the eastern lowland is the largest. It has a very dark black coat, similar to the mountain gorilla, but its hair is shorter on the head and body.

Although it can be hard to tell them apart, eastern lowland gorillas have larger hands, stockier bodies and shorter noses than other gorilla species.

Eastern lowland gorillas are very gentle and sociable creatures. They usually live in troops with between 2 and 30+ other gorillas.

The diet of a lowland gorilla is quite different to the mountain gorilla. Around two-thirds of their diet consists of fruits, while the rest is plants.

As well as poaching and habitat loss, bushmeat hunting is a massive threat to the eastern lowland gorilla. This is when local, often poor, people hunt wild animals for food.

An infant eastern lowland gorilla in Kahuzi-Biega National Park. *Photo by Joe Mckenna*

Male mountain gorilla.

Mountain Gorilla

Scientific name: *Gorilla beringei beringei*

There are two populations of mountain gorilla: one group lives in the Virunga volcanic mountains of Central Africa, and the other in Bwindi Impenetrable National Park, Uganda.

They live in high forests, usually between 8,000-13,000 ft (2400-4000m).

There are only around 1063 mountain gorillas living in the wild, and they are listed as endangered.

They are smaller than the eastern lowland gorilla, and their coats are much thicker and warmer as they live in a cooler climate.

Mountain gorillas are **diurnal**, meaning they spend most of their day eating and sleep at night.

Around 80 per cent of the mountain gorillas diet is made up of shoots and leaves, as there is not much fruit at high altitudes for them to eat. However, they love eating and spend around a quarter of their day doing it!

A female mountain gorilla with her infant.

From Birth to Adulthood

Let's learn more about the early life of gorillas.

Baby gorillas are called **infants**.

• • •

When they are born, infants are smaller than humans. They weigh between 3-4 lbs. (1.4-1.8kg).

• • •

The gestation period (how long she is pregnant) of a female gorilla is 8.5 months.

A young gorilla in the
Democratic Republic of Congo.

Despite being smaller than humans, they grow much faster than us. They are fully grown adults when they are 12 years old.

• • •

Mothers and infants stay very close together for around five to six months.

• • •

At just eight weeks old they will start playing and jumping around.

At around three months old, they will start to hold objects and move around more, and at eight months old they will walk further away from their mothers and become more adventurous.

• • •

Infants drink their mother's milk until they are around three years old.

• • •

They will start to eat some plants when they are around 2.5 months old, and increasingly eat more over the next few months.

Once a young gorilla can explore on its own, they will usually be accompanied by their siblings or other juveniles.

• • •

Silverbacks often don't know which infants are theirs, as there are often several silverbacks and females in one group, but they still help with taking care of them.

• • •

Female gorillas usually give birth every four years.

Like all primates, most of the time,
gorillas will only give birth to one infant.
Twins can happen, but it's very rare.

• • •

It can be hard to tell the males and
females apart when they are young.
But, as the male gorillas age, their grey
backs start forming. Males get their
silverbacks around 13 years of age.

Their Daily Lives

What do gorillas do all day?!

Gorillas walk **quadrilaterally**, meaning they use all four limbs for walking. They walk on their knuckles, which helps to support the weight of their head and upper body.

• • •

Gorillas can be seen showing human emotions, such as sadness and affection towards others.

A male mountain gorilla in Uganda.

Female mountain gorilla with her infant.

Gorillas are mostly **herbivores**, which means they eat plants and leaves. However they may also eat insects such as ants from time to time.

• • •

Gorillas are big creatures, so they need a lot of food. Male gorillas may eat up to 66 lbs (30 kg) of food a day, while females can eat 40 lbs (18 kg).

• • •

Gorillas aren't territorial and several troops may live in the same area of land without problems. However, if a silverback feels threatened he can become violent to defend his troop.

Gorillas groom each other regularly, which helps to improve the bond between them. It is an important part of their socializing routine.

• • •

Every day, gorillas build a new nest to sleep in that night. Each gorilla will build its own nest, except for infants who will stay with their mothers.

• • •

In 2005, gorillas were observed using a stick to measure the depth of some muddy water. This shows just how intelligent they are—even in the wild away from human influence.

Gorillas have their own language. They use a wide range of different sounds to communicate with each other.

• • •

Although movies like *King Kong* may make you think that gorillas can be aggressive, they are some of the most peaceful wild animals. Even when confronted with danger they will try to solve the problem calmly before getting aggressive.

Young mountain gorillas.

Famous Gorillas

There are hundreds of gorillas featured in music, TV shows, films and books. They are a popular character! So let's take a look at just a few of the most famous ones.

Magilla Gorilla was a fictional character in a cartoon series of the same name. The series was by the same creator as The Flintstones. Magilla Gorilla makes an appearance in a follow-up series called *The Flintstones and Friends.*

A poster for the 1933 King Kong movie.

King Kong and Mighty Joe Young are two of the most famous fictional gorillas. The latest Godzilla movie was released in March 2021: *Godzilla vs. Kong*, but there are dozens of others.

Magilla Gorilla. *Copyright: Hanna Barbara*

Pittsburg State University's mascot is a gorilla. It is the only public college in the USA with a gorilla mascot.

• • •

The mascot of the Phoenix Suns NBA team is also a gorilla.

• • •

Tony O'Shea, a famous British darts player has the nickname 'Silverback', because of the way he crouches over when he takes his turn!

There is a stage show called *A Young Man Dressed As A Gorilla Dressed As An Old Man Sits Rocking In A Rocking Chair for 56 Minutes and Then Leaves*, which is simply a man in a gorilla costume doing exactly what the title says. Would you watch it?!

• • •

Koko the gorilla was born at San Francisco Zoo in 1971. She was one of the world's most famous gorillas. She recognized over 2,000 spoken English words and 1,000 symbols from 'Gorilla Sign Language' — approximately the same as a three-year-old child.

Koko with one of her pet cats, Ms Gray.

Image: The Gorilla Foundation.

A poster for the 1998 *Gorillas in the Mist* movie. *Copyright: Universal Pictures*

Koko the gorilla met many celebrities before her death in 2018, including Robin Williams, Leonardo DiCaprio and Sting.

• • •

The 1988 movie, *Gorillas in the Mist*, was about the gorilla conservation activist called Dian Fossey. It's a beautiful movie and taught the world more about gorillas.

The Future

From poaching to Ebola, life is tough for gorillas.

There are only around 200,000 gorillas still living in the wild, making them one of the most endangered ape species.

• • •

All gorilla species are either **endangered** or **critically endangered**. This means that without conservation efforts they may become extinct.

West lowland silverback gorilla.

Humans are the biggest threat to gorillas. Destruction of their habitats and poaching means their numbers are declining.

• • •

Fortunately, many conservation organizations are working to help gorillas and prevent them from extinction.

• • •

The Great Apes Survival Project was founded in 2001 and has already formed the **Gorilla Agreement**, an international treaty to help protect gorilla populations.

As humans start building further up the mountains, mountain gorillas are forced to move even higher where it is colder and more dangerous for them.

• • •

There are many ways that you can help to protect gorillas. Organizations such as *Virunga National Park* and *WWF* allow you to adopt gorillas for a small fee each month. All money goes to their conservation efforts.

And of course, just spreading awareness of the problems they face, on social media or in person, is a great way to help!

Other Fun Facts

More reasons to love gorillas.

Gorillas have unique nose prints, just like humans have unique fingerprints!

• • •

Gorillas are **neophobic**. This means they are very sensitive to even small environmental changes.

• • •

World Gorilla Day is celebrated every year on 24th September.

At Atlanta Zoo in 2020, the zookeepers organized a gorilla Easter egg hunt. They hid eggs made of Jell-o and other tasty snacks for the western lowland gorillas to find.

Why are there eastern and western gorillas? The River Congo is the most likely reason, as it separates the two species habitats.

• • •

Gorillas don't have tails.

• • •

Gorillas rarely drink water. Instead, they get their water from the plants they eat.

It is possible to see gorillas in the wild in countries such as Uganda and Rwanda on guided treks. However, these are strictly monitored so you never get too close to them, as it would stress them out.

• • •

The average gorilla is around six times stronger than the average human. As they use their upper bodies for moving around, their muscles are very strong.

• • •

Gorillas will occasionally eat soil and ash as it helps with digestion.

A person who studies gorillas and other primates is called a **primatologist**.

• • •

Mountain gorillas have a natural fear of some insects and reptiles! Young gorillas will jump when they see a chameleon, for example. This is something that still baffles scientists.

Gorilla *quiz*

Now test your knowledge in our Gorilla Quiz! Answers are on page 81.

1. What do you call a person who studies primates?

2. What are young male gorillas called?

3. How many different species of primates are there?

4. Can you name the different species and subspecies of gorilla?

5. What are baby gorillas called?

A young male mountain gorilla.

6. What do you call a group of gorillas?

7. Where can you find Eastern lowland gorillas?

8. Which is the smallest species of gorilla?

9. How often do female gorillas give birth?

10. Gorillas can show human emotions. True or false?

11. What is the biggest threat to gorillas?

12. What is the scientific name for the Western gorilla?

13. How old was Fatou, the oldest known gorilla, when she died?

14. What do you call the male leader of a troop of gorillas?

15. How long do gorillas live for in the wild?

16. Mountain gorillas are diurnal. What does this mean?

17. Gorillas build a new sleeping nest every night. True or false?

18. What percentage of the mountain gorilla's diet consists of fruit?

19. What date is World Gorilla Day?

20. Gorillas love drinking from rivers. True or false?

Answers:

1. Primatologist.

2. Black backs.

3. Eight.

4. Western gorilla (Cross River gorilla and Western lowland gorilla); Eastern gorilla (Eastern lowland gorilla and Mountain gorilla).

5. Infants.

6. A troop.

7. In the tropical rainforests of the Democratic Republic of Congo.

8. Western lowland gorilla.

9. Usually every four years.

10. True!

11. Humans.

12. Gorilla gorilla.

13. 62 years old.

14. A silverback.

15. Around 25-30 years.

16. They are awake during the day, and sleep at night.

17. True.

18. 20%.

19. 24th September.

20. False. They rarely drink water.

Gorilla
Word search

```
A G F D S A I V J H G F
S B O T R E S N V C X Y
I A F R I C A N F B M J
L V K Z I X Q E F A N H
V D I D S L F H J K N F
E S N W B V L X E F T T
R K G R E A T A P E R Y
B I K T W S B F D S S T
A U O R D Z T K J G F R
C G N E A S T E R N V E
K F G D F G H J R N B S
N M O U N T A I N N C F
```

Can you find all the words below in the wordsearch puzzle on the left?

AFRICA   GREAT APE   WESTERN

GORILLA   INFANT   EASTERN

MOUNTAIN   SILVERBACK   KING KONG

Solution

	G					I				
S		O					N			
I	A	F	R	I	C	A		F		
L	K		I					A		
V	I			L					N	
E	N	W		L						T
R	G	R	E	A	T	A	P	E		
B	K		S							
A	O			T						
C	N	E	A	S	T	E	R	N		
K	G						R			
	M	O	U	N	T	A	I	N	N	

Sources

"Oldest Living Gorilla In Captivity". 2019. Guinness World Records. https://www.guinnessworldrecords.com/world-records/89861-oldest-living-gorilla-in-captivity

"A Carthaginian Exploration of the West African Coast". Archived from the original on 14 March 2017.

"Gorilla - Wikipedia". 2021. En.Wikipedia.Org. https://en.wikipedia.org/wiki/Gorilla.

"Western Lowland Gorilla - Wikipedia". 2021. En.Wikipedia.Org. https://en.wikipedia.org/wiki/Western_lowland_gorilla.

"Types Of Gorillas". 2021. Home.Adelphi.Edu. https://home.adelphi.edu/~al21824/Types%20of%20Gorillas.html#:~:text=Western%20Lowland%20Gorilla,-The%20Western%20Lowland&text=Compared%20to%20other%20subspecies%2C%20they,the%20last%2020%2D25%20years.

"Mountain Gorilla - Wikipedia". 2021. En.Wikipedia.Org. https://en.wikipedia.org/wiki/Mountain_gorilla.

"Animals: Gorilla". 2021. Ducksters.Com. https://www.ducksters.com/animals/gorilla.php.

"What Is A Baby Gorilla Called? Baby Gorilla". 2020. Wild Gorilla Safaris. https://www.wildgorillasafaris.com/facts-about-gorilla-facts/what-is-a-baby-gorilla-called/.

"All About The Gorilla - Birth & Care Of Young| Seaworld Parks & Entertainment". 2021. Seaworld. Org. https://seaworld.org/animals/all-about/gorilla/care-of-young/#:~:text=Females%20usually%20give%20birth%20around,6%20offspring%20in%20a%20lifetime.

A-Z, Animals, Animal 10s, Most Endangered, Highest Jumpers, Longest Living, Endangered Change, and Unusual Habits et al. 2021. "Amazing Facts About Gorillas | Onekindplanet Animal Education & Facts". Onekindplanet. https://onekindplanet.org/animal/gorilla/.

"Koko (Gorilla) - Wikipedia". 2021. En.Wikipedia.Org. https://en.wikipedia.org/wiki/Koko_(gorilla).

"10 Facts About Gorillas". 2021. FOUR PAWS International - Animal Welfare Organisation. https://www.four-paws.org/campaigns-topics/topics/help-for-orangutans/10-facts-about-gorillas.

"50 Interesting Facts About Gorillas". 2019. Green Global Travel. https://greenglobaltravel.com/facts-about-gorillas/.

We hope you learned some awesome facts about gorillas! We'd love it if you left a review—they always make us smile :)

Follow us at www.bellanovabooks.com for monthly book giveaways and more!

Also by Jenny Kellett

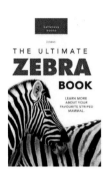

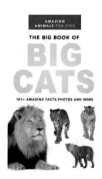

... and more!

Available in all major online bookstores

Made in the USA
Las Vegas, NV
18 January 2024

84541645R00055